Happy Christmas

CW01646557

Enjoy creating new dishes with Tarla Dalal. Very interesting recipes. Hope you like and enjoy cooking

Love
Bhanumati
&
Bhikhukaka
xx

Kebabs & Tikkis

Tarla Dalal
INDIA'S #1 COOKERY AUTHOR

COOK BOOKS BY TARLA DALAL

Second Printing : 2009

ISBN : 978-81-89491-77-2

Price Rs. 250/-

Published & Distributed by :
SANJAY & COMPANY
353/A-1, Shah & Nahar Industrial Estate, Dhanraj Mill Compound, Lower Parel (W), Mumbai - 400 013. INDIA.
Tel. : (91-22) 4345 2400 • Fax : (91-22) 2496 5876 • E-mail : sanjay@tarladalal.com • Website : www.tarladalal.com

Recipe Research & Production Design
Arati Fedane
Ritika Rajpal

Nutritionist
Nisha Katira
Sapna Kamdar

Photography
Payal Choksi

Copy Editor
Janani Gopalakrishnan

Design
Satyamangal Rege

Typesetting
Adityas Enterprises

Printed by
Minal Sales Agencies, Mumbai

introduction

I love entertaining and having parties, like most of you. And when I talk to fellow-hosts, I find that they are almost always worried about what snacks to serve the main course and desserts are easier to finalise! It so happens that after much thought they usually settle for common, tried-and-tested dishes such as Paneer Tikkas. Hmmm, there will be a time when your guests would have had enough of it!

Keeping this in mind, I present Kebabs and Tikkis A compilation of 61 delicious and innovative kebab, tikka and tikki recipes. For those of you who are willing to look beyond Indian snacks, I have also included a section of my all-time favourite international finger foods.

Some of the kebabs have been deep-fried or cooked in ghee. You could shallow-fry these or use oil instead of ghee, so that you can rest assured on the health front too. And well, there is something for everybody, from the live-for-the-day eater to the more discerning health-conscious ones.

That said, variety alone does not ensure that the starters/snacks served during your party become a huge hit with the guests. A major part of the planning involves combining these snacks appropriately into what is today popular-known as a "platter". Platters are a dominant phenomenon today they ensure guests a well-

chosen selection of snacks replete with rotis, a salad or two and suitable chutneys and sauces. A well-planned platter is wholesome and nutritious and capable of serving as a meal in itself for the snack-lover (while serving as a starter for the rest).

This book comes replete with 10 platter suggestions that guide you on how to serve your tikkis, tikkas and kebabs, and the accompaniments that we feel they would ideally combine with. These platters are based on specific themes. Plus, there is a second index included in this book which categories the recipes according to type this enables you to exercise your imagination to come up with your own platter options too... and I'm sure those will be a success too. Innovation is the key!

In the coming pages, you will discover yummy tikkis such as Mutter aur Phudine ki Tikki, page 33, Dahi Saunfiyani Tikki, page 34 and Chick Pea and Soya Tikki, page 32, an array of mouth-watering kebabs such as Badam aur Arbi ke Kebab, page 14, Vegetable Shikampuri Kebab, page 76 and Corn Seekh Kebab, page 18, and a delectable variety of soft and creamy tikkas such as Pahadi Paneer Tikka, page 25, Makhmali Paneer Tikka, page 26 and Tilwale Aloo ka Tikka, page 58.

For those who wish for a taste of the world, there are international favourites such as Aloo Cheese Croquettes, page 69, Sweet Corn Balls, page 43 and Paneer, Mushroom and Capsicum Satay, page 44. Accompaniments such as Phudina Chutney, page 20, Peanut Sauce, page 48 and Chunky Vegetable Dip, page 94 duly complement the snacks, enhancing their appeal. Go ahead and put together one of the recommended platters or come up with an original platter full of your favourite recipes, Indian and beyond!

The next time you plan a party or are attacked by a sudden hunger pang, fret not, and just pull out this book. Prepare some of these easy-to-follow recipes and watch the platters empty while the diners' faces light up!

Happy entertaining,

Tarla Dalal

platters

Seekh Kebab Platter

Paneer Platter

Crispy Tikki Platter

platters

Oriental Platter

All Time Favourite

Continental Platter

Nawabi Platter

platters

Low Cal Kebab Platter

kebabs &tikkis

Kebab Ka Khazana

Tasty Tikkis

Melt In Your Mouth Tikkas

International Favourites

accompaniments

Rotis & Breads

Chutneys

Sauce & Dips

Salads

Basic Recipe

Seekh Kebab *platter*

Seekh kebabs are traditional *kebabs* that originated in Afghanistan. The uniqueness of this variety lies in the method of preparation, wherein the prepared *kebab* mixture is pressed onto a thick metal skewer known as a *seekh*. This *seekh* is then placed into a tandoor that gives the *kebab* a delicious smoky flavour. Most people associate *seekh kebabs* with meat. However, nearly any vegetable when combined with a binding agent like cornflour, potato or bread can make great *seekh kebabs*. Interestingly, you need not look anywhere outside your kitchen for this seemingly exotic class of *kebabs*! They can be prepared in your own kitchen if you have an electric grill or barbeque. If you don't have *seekhs* or metal skewers you can use wooden pencils and grill the *kebabs* over the flame. Bread sticks make great edible skewers, and are an instant hit with kids. For best results, ensure that the *seekh* is greased before you press the *kebab* mixture onto it.

This section provides a great combination of *seekh kebabs* that can be served together as a platter while entertaining or for your own family.

Suran Chana Dal Seekh Kebab
Badam aur Arbi ke Kebab
Moong Dal Seekh Kebab
Corn Seekh Kebab
Tava Roti
Phudina Chutney
Kachumber

Suran Chana Dal Seekh Kebab

Yam or suran combined with chana dal and a mélange of spices makes an interesting seekh kebab that tastes fantastic.

Preparation Time: 15 minutes.
Cooking Time: 30 minutes.
Makes 8 pieces.

3 tbsp oil
½ cup *chana dal* (split Bengal gram)
1½ cups finely chopped yam (*suran*)
½ cup thinly sliced onions
1½ tsp grated ginger (*adrak*)
1 tsp finely chopped garlic (*lehsun*)
2 tsp finely chopped green chillies
¼ cup chopped mint leaves (*phudina*)
1 tbsp *chaat masala*
¼ tsp *garam masala*
Salt to taste
Oil for brushing

1. Heat 1 tbsp of oil in a pan, add the *chana dal* and sauté it till it turns light pink in colour.
2. Cool and grind the *chana dal* in a mixer to a powder. Keep aside.
3. Heat the remaining 2 tbsp of oil in another pan, add the onions, ginger, garlic and green chillies and sauté till the onions turn translucent.
4. Add the yam and cook over a slow flame for 5 to 7 minutes.
5. Add ½ cup of water, cover and cook till the yam is soft and all the moisture has evaporated.
6. Cool, add the mint leaves and blend in a mixer to a coarse paste without using any water.
7. Transfer this mixture to a bowl, add the *chana dal* powder, *chaat masala*, *garam masala* and salt and mix well.
8. Divide the mixture into 2 equal portions and using a thick *seekh* (metal skewer), press each portion of the mixture on it with your fingers to make a 200 mm. (8") long *kebab*.
9. Brush each *kebab* with a little oil and cook them over a charcoal or electric barbeque till they are evenly browned on all sides (approx. 3 to 4 minutes).
10. Cut each *kebab* into 4 equal pieces and serve hot.

Badam aur Arbi ke Kebab

Rich and delicious, this is the perfect preparation to woo your guests with!

Preparation Time: 15 minutes.
Cooking Time: 15 minutes.
Makes 4 kebabs.

For the almond paste

½ tbsp ghee
¼ cup sliced onions
1 tbsp blanched and peeled almonds (*badam*)
1 tbsp cashewnuts (*kaju*)

Other ingredients

1 tbsp ghee
½ tsp ginger-garlic (*adrak-lehsun*) paste
1 tsp finely chopped green chillies
¾ cup boiled, peeled and mashed colocasia (*arbi*)
½ tsp cardamom (*elaichi*) powder
1 tsp chilli powder
A pinch nutmeg (*jaiphal*) powder
A few strands saffron (kesar)
1 tbsp khoya (*mava*)
1 tbsp roasted *chana dal* (*dariya dal*) powder
3 to 4 blanched and peeled almonds (badam), broken into pieces
Salt to taste
1 piece coal, for smoking
Oil for brushing

For the almond paste

1. Heat the ghee in a pan, add the onions and sauté for a minute.
2. Add the almonds and cashewnuts and sauté till the onions turn translucent. Allow it to cool.
3. Blend in a mixer to a smooth paste and keep aside.

How to proceed

1. Heat the ghee in a pan, add the ginger-garlic paste and sauté for a minute.
2. Add the green chillies and colocasia, mix well and sauté for another 2 minutes.
3. Remove from the flame and keep aside to cool.
4. Add all the remaining ingredients including the almond paste and mix well.
5. Heat the coal and carefully place it in a bowl. Place this bowl in the pan with the colocasia mixture and cover the pan with a lid. Keep aside for 30 minutes.
6. Divide the mixture into 4 equal portions and using a thick *seekh* (metal skewer), press each portion of the mixture on it with your fingers to make a 100 mm. (4") long *kebab*.
7. Brush each *kebab* very lightly with oil and cook them over the grill or over a charcoal barbeque till the *kebabs* are evenly browned (approx. 3 to 4 minutes) on all sides.
   Serve hot.

Moong Dal Seekh Kebab

A thoughtful combination of yellow *moong dal*, mashed potatoes and a range of spices is pressed onto a *seekh* and cooked to perfection on a grill.

Preparation Time: 10 minutes.
Cooking Time: 30 minutes.
Makes 8 pieces.

1 cup yellow *moong dal* (split yellow gram)
1 cup boiled, peeled and grated potatoes
3 tbsp grated onions
2 tsp chilli powder
¼ tsp *garam masala*
¼ tsp turmeric powder (*haldi*)
1 tsp ginger-garlic (*adrak-lehsun*) paste
2 tsp chaat masala
2 tbsp chopped coriander (*dhania*)
Salt to taste
Ghee for brushing

1. Clean, wash and boil the *moong dal* in 1 cup of water till the *dal* is soft and cooked and all the water has evaporated.
2. Combine the cooked *dal* with all the remaining ingredients and mix well.
3. Divide the mixture into 4 equal portions and using a thick *seekh* (metal skewer), press each portion of the *dal* mixture on it with your fingers to make a 100 mm. (4") long *kebab*.
4. Brush each *kebab* with a little ghee and cook them over a charcoal or electric barbeque till they are evenly browned on all sides (approx. 3 to 4 minutes).
5. Cut each *kebab* into 2 pieces and serve hot.

Corn Seekh Kebab

Mouth-watering sweet corn *seekh* kebabs brushed with warm chilli butter while grilling, this is truly a tongue-thriller!

Preparation Time: 10 minutes.
Cooking Time: 10 minutes.
Makes 4 kebabs.

1 cup boiled, peeled and mashed potatoes
¼ cup grated sweet corn (*makai ke dane*)
2 tbsp finely chopped spring onion whites
1 tbsp finely chopped green chillies
1 tbsp cornflour
Salt to taste
½ tsp *garam masala*
2 tsp ghee
2 tsp melted butter mixed with 2 tsp chilli powder for brushing

1. Combine all the ingredients, except the ghee, in a bowl and mix well. Keep aside.
2. Heat the ghee in a pan and add the prepared mixture and cook for 2 to 3 minutes. Allow the mixture to cool.
3. Divide the mixture into 4 equal portions and using a thick *seekh* (metal skewer), press each portion of the mixture on it with your fingers to make a 100 mm. (4") long *kebab*.
4. Brush each *kebab* with the butter mixture and cook them over a charcoal or electric barbeque till they are evenly browned on all sides (approx. 3 to 4 minutes).
   Serve hot.

Tava Roti

This basic *roti* is worth being called a truly universal accompaniment it goes well with practically all dishes!

Preparation Time: 5 - 7 minutes.
Cooking Time: 15 minutes.
Makes 6 rotis.

1 cup whole wheat flour (*gehun ka atta*)

½ tsp salt

1 tsp oil

Whole wheat flour (*gehun ka atta*) for rolling

Ghee for topping

1. Combine the flour and salt and knead into a soft and pliable dough.
2. Add the oil and knead again till it is smooth and elastic.
3. Cover and keep aside for 10 to 15 minutes.
4. Divide the dough into 6 equal portions.
5. Roll out each portion, using a little flour, into approx. 150 mm. (6") diameter circles. Dust wheat flour as required to facilitate even rolling.

6. Dust off any excess wheat flour and place the *roti* on a hot *tava* (griddle).
7. Turn over in a few seconds and cook this side till the edges begin to curl slightly and small blisters appear on the surface.
8. Cook the other side for a few more seconds.
9. Lift the *roti* with a pair of flat tongs and roast on both sides over an open flame till it puffs up.
10. Flatten the *roti* and apply some ghee on top.
11. Repeat to make 5 more *rotis*.

Serve hot.

Phudina Chutney

This pungent accompaniment will surely please your taste-buds.

Preparation Time: 10 minutes.
Cooking Time: Nil.
Makes 1 cup.

2 cups chopped mint leaves (*phudina*)
1 cup chopped coriander (*dhania*)
1 large onion, sliced (optional)
2 tbsp lemon juice
1 tbsp sugar
4 green chillies, roughly chopped
12 mm. (½") piece ginger (*adrak*)
Salt to taste

1. Combine all the ingredients and blend in a mixer to a smooth paste using a little water if required.
2. Refrigerate and use as required.

Kachumber

Simple but exciting-nothing describes kachumber better!

Preparation Time: 10 minutes.
Cooking Time: Nil.
Serves 4.

½ cup chopped onions

½ cup chopped cucumber

½ cup chopped tomatoes

½ tbsp lemon juice

Salt to taste

2 tbsp chopped coriander (dhania)

1. Combine all the ingredients in a serving bowl and mix well.
2. Refrigerate and serve chilled.

No vegetarian meal is complete without *paneer* or cottage cheese. *Paneer* is one of the most widely used ingredients in preparing vegetarian *tikkas*. Its unique ability to absorb the flavour of any marinade makes it an ideal choice. Its rich and creamy texture and great appearance add to its merits. The *paneer* platter brings together several all-time favourite *paneer tikkas* on your dining table. Serve this platter with *laccha* onions, that is, onions that have been sliced and pickled in vinegar or lime juice and flavoured with fresh mint leaves, sliced radish etc. You could also buy readymade *naan* or *tandoori roti*, cut it into small triangles and serve with the *kebabs* if you are in a rush.

Paneer platter

Makhmali Paneer Tikka

True to its name, this *tikka* will melt in your mouth, delighting your taste buds!

Preparation Time: 10 minutes.
Cooking Time: 10 minutes.
Serves 4.
Baking Temperature: 200°C (400°F).
Baking Time: 20 minutes.

3 cups *paneer* (cottage cheese), cut into 50 mm. (2") cubes

To be mixed into a marinade

¾ cup thick fresh hung curds *dahi*)
¼ cup cheese spread
1 tsp green chilli paste
2 tbsp cashewnut (*kaju*) powder
½ tsp *garam masala*
Salt to taste

1. Combine the *paneer* cubes with the prepared marinade and toss gently till the paste coats the *paneer* pieces evenly from all sides. Keep aside for 15 minutes.
2. Arrange the *paneer* pieces on the wire rack in a pre-heated oven at 200°C (400°F) and grill till the *paneer* is done (approx. 15 minutes).
3. Remove from the oven and serve hot.

Paneer Amritsari Tikka

A vegetarian adaptation of the traditional Punjabi favourite — the Fish Amritsari. You can avoid the food colour if you wish.

Preparation Time: 10 minutes.
Cooking Time: 15 minutes.
Serves 4.

To be mixed into a marinade

2 tbsp ginger-garlic (*adrak-lehsun*) paste
½ tsp carom seeds (*ajwain*)
A few drops of orange food colour
Salt to taste
½ tsp chilli powder

Other ingredients

2 cups *paneer* (cottage cheese), cut into 2" x ½" x ½" strips
4-5 tbsp *besan* (Bengal gram flour), dry roasted
Oil for deep-frying
1 tbsp *chaat masala* for sprinkling

1. Combine the *paneer* strips with the prepared marinade and toss gently till the marinade coats the *paneer* strips evenly from all sides. Keep aside for 15 minutes.
2. Sprinkle *besan* on the marinated *paneer* strips and mix gently so that the *besan* coats the *paneer* evenly from all sides.
3. Heat the oil in a *kadhai* on a medium flame and deep-fry the *paneer* pieces till golden brown. Drain on absorbent paper.
Serve hot sprinkled with *chaat masala.*

Garlic Naan

Exquisitely flavoured leavened bread cooked in a *tandoor*! I have added some garlic cloves to the *naan* dough to enhance its flavour.

Preparation Time: 15 minutes.
Cooking Time: 15 minutes.
Makes 6 naans.

To be ground into a coarse paste

¼ cup garlic (*lehsun*) cloves, peeled
1 tsp cumin seeds (*jeera)*
2 green chillies, finely chopped
1 tbsp lemon juice
1 tsp sugar

Other ingredients

1 cup plain flour (*maida)*
½ tsp fresh yeast, crumbled
½ tsp sugar
1 tbsp oil
½ tsp salt
Oil for greasing
Butter for brushing for serving

1. Dissolve the yeast and sugar in 2 tbsp of lukewarm water and leave aside for 10 minutes or until the yeast begins to ferment.
2. Combine all the ingredients including the ground paste in a bowl and knead into a soft dough, using enough water until it is smooth and elastic (approx. 5 to 7 minutes).
3. Cover the dough with a wet muslin cloth and keep aside till it doubles in volume (approx.15 to 20 minutes).
4. Press the dough lightly to remove the air.
5. Divide the dough into 4 equal portions and roll out each portion into a 100 mm. (4") diameter circle.
6. Grease a pressure cooker very lightly with oil. Remove the lid from the pressure cooker and heat it upside down over an open flame.
7. Apply a little water on one side of each *naan* and stick the wet side of the *naan* around the inside of the pressure cooker.
8. Place the pressure cooker upside down directly on the surface and cook till both sides are golden brown. You can apply 3 to 4 *naans* at a time inside the walls of the pressure cooker.
9. Remove the *naans* and brush with butter. Serve hot.

Dahiwali Phudina Chutney

An interesting combination of curds and *phudina chutney*, which shall surely (hyper)activate your gastronomic juices!

Preparation Time: 5 minutes.
Cooking Time: Nil.
Makes 1 cup.

¾ cup fresh curds (*dahi*), whisked
¼ cup *phudina chutney*, page 19
Salt to taste

1. Combine all the ingredients in a bowl and mix well.
2. Store refrigerated in an air-tight container and use as required.

Laccha Onions

An excellent value-add to any kebab platter.

Preparation Time: A few minutes.
Cooking Time: Nil.
Makes 1 cup.

1 cup onion rings
1 tbsp vinegar or lemon juice
Salt to taste

1. Put the onion rings into a bowl of ice-cold water and keep aside for 15-20 minutes. This will make them crisp.
2. When ready to serve, drain, put on a kitchen towel and pat dry.
3. Add the vinegar and salt and mix gently. Serve immediately.

Mint Sprigs

Remove the topmost leaves of mint (*phudina*) and put them in ice-cold water. When ready to serve, drain, put on a kitchen towel and pat dry.

Red Radish Slices

Cut 4-5 slices of radish (*mooli*) and put them in ice-cold water. When ready to serve, drain, place on a kitchen towel and pat dry.

Crispy TIKKI platter

A platter of assorted deep-fried *tikkis* is sure to captivate the hearts of young and old alike surely, it's worth setting diet plans aside for this! Nowadays, people tend to condemn all deep fried foods as bad, but it is not harmful to indulge in these crispy treats occasionally. *Chick Pea and Soya Tikki*, for instance, has nourishing ingredients and can be made healthier if cooked on a *tava* (griddle). *Mutter aur Phudine ki Tikki* is another traditional combo that will never fail to impress the diners! *Dahi Saunfiyani Tikki* is a Mughlai specialty made using hung curds, which has a really unique fragrance. *Aloo Methi Tikki*, of course, needs no introduction. Indulge in this collection of ever-popular crispy *tikkis*!

Chick Pea and Soya Tikki

Soya granules combined with *kabuli chana* for binding, make simple yet scrumptious *tikkis*.

Preparation Time: 10 minutes.
Cooking Time: 10 minutes.
Makes 8 to 10 tikkis.
Soaking Time: Overnight.

½ cup *kabuli chana* (chick peas)
½ cup soya granules
1 tbsp finely chopped mint leaves (*phudina*)
1 tsp finely chopped green chillies
1 tsp finely chopped ginger (*adrak*)
Salt to taste
Oil for deep-frying

1. Clean, wash and soak the *kabuli chana* overnight.
2. Drain, add 2 cups of water and pressure cook for 3 to 4 whistles or until the *kabuli chana* is cooked.
3. Allow the steam to escape before opening the lid.
4. Drain out all the excess water and keep the *kabuli chana* aside.
5. Soak the soya granules in hot water for 10 to 15 minutes. Drain and squeeze out all the water.
6. Combine the soya granules, *kabuli chana*, mint leaves, green chillies, ginger and salt and blend in a mixer to a coarse paste.
7. Divide the mixture into 8 to 10 equal portions and shape each portion into round, flat *tikki*.
8. Heat the oil in a *kadhai* on a medium flame and deep-fry the *tikkis* till they are golden brown in colour from both sides. Drain on an absorbent paper and serve hot.

Mutter aur Phudine ki Tikki

Green peas make great *tikkis* when combined with potatoes and a handful of mint leaves.

Preparation Time: 5 minutes.
Cooking Time: 10 minutes.
Makes 8 to 10 tikkis.

1 cup boiled green peas
½ cup boiled, peeled and mashed potatoes
2 tbsp chopped mint leaves (*phudina*)
Salt to taste
1½ tsp *garam masala*
2 green chillies, finely chopped
Oil for deep-frying

1. Combine all the ingredients and blend in a mixer to a coarse mixture (Add a little water if required).
2. Divide the mixture into 8 to 10 equal portions and shape each portion into a round *tikki*.
3. Heat the oil in a *kadhai* on a medium flame and deep-fry the *tikkis* till they are golden brown in colour from all sides. Drain on an absorbent paper and serve hot.

Dahi Saunfiyani Tikki

Enjoy these tangy *tikkis* flavoured in true Mughlai style!

Preparation Time: 15 minutes.
Cooking Time: 15 minutes.
Makes 8 tikkis.

1 cup hung curds (*dahi*)
½ cup grated *paneer* (*cottage cheese*)
3 tsp finely chopped green chillies
½ tsp chopped garlic (*lehsun*)
A pinch sugar
Salt to taste
2 tbsp finely chopped coriander (*dhania*)
2 tbsp finely chopped mint leaves (*phudina*)
1 tsp fennel seeds (*saunf*) powder
1 tbsp ghee
2 tbsp roasted *chana dal* (*dariya dal*) powder
2 tsp cornflour
Oil for deep-frying

1. Combine the curds, *paneer*, green chillies, garlic, sugar, salt, coriander, mint leaves and fennel seeds powder in a bowl and mix well. Keep aside.
2. Heat the ghee in a pan, add the roasted *chana dal* powder, curds mixture and cornflour and cook till the mixture thickens and starts to leave the sides of the pan. Keep aside to cool.
3. Divide the mixture into 8 equal portions and shape each portion into a round, flat *tikki*.
4. Heat the oil in a *kadhai* on a medium flame and deep-fry the *tikkis* till they are golden brown in colour from both sides. Drain on absorbent paper and serve hot.

Aloo Methi ki Tikki

The ever popular combination of fenugreek leaves and potatoes now in a *tikki* form!

Preparation Time: 15 minutes.
Cooking Time: 15 minutes.
Makes 8 tikkis.

2 tsp oil
1 tsp cumin seeds (*jeera*)
2 tsp finely chopped green chillies
½ tsp finely chopped ginger (*adrak*)
¼ cup chopped onions
1 cup boiled and mashed potatoes
½ cup chopped fenugreek (*methi*) leaves
3 tsp dried fenugreek leaves (*kasuri methi*), dry roasted and crushed
2 tsp dry mango powder (*amchur*)
½ tsp turmeric powder (*haldi*)
½ tsp *garam masala*
Salt to taste
¼ cup chopped coriander (*dhania*)
¼ cup bread crumbs for rolling
Oil for deep frying

1. Heat the oil in a pan and add the cumin seeds.
2. When they crackle, add the green chilies, ginger and onions and sauté for 2 to 3 minutes or till the onions turn translucent.
3. Add all the remaining ingredients, mix well and sauté for 2 minutes.
4. Remove from the flame and allow the mixture to cool.
5. Divide the mixture into 8 equal portions and shape each portion into a round, flat *tikki*.
6. Roll each *tikki* in bread crumbs in such a way that the *tikkis* are evenly coated from both sides.
7. Heat the oil in a *kadhai* on a medium flame and deep-fry the *tikkis* till they are golden brown in colour from both sides. Drain on absorbent paper and serve hot.

Rumali Roti

A traditional roti that is a little difficult to make at home. Roll out as thinly as possible and stretch before cooking.

Preparation Time: 10 minutes.
Cooking Time: 20 minutes.
Makes 10 to 15 rotis.

2½ cups plain flour (*maida*)
Salt to taste
2 pinches soda bi-carb
Milk for kneading
plain flour (*maida*) for rolling

1. Combine the flour, salt and soda bi-carb in a bowl and knead into a soft dough using enough milk. Keep aside for 1 hour.
2. Knead again, divide into 10 to 15 portions and roll out each portion very thinly using a little flour.
3. Place a wok upside down on a flame.
4. Stretch the *roti* a little on all sides and put on the upside down wok and cook till done. Serve hot.

Khajur Imli ki Chutney

A khatti mithi chutney usually eaten with chaat.

Preparation Time: 15 minutes.
Cooking Time: 10 minutes.
Makes 2 cups.

2 cups deseeded dates (*khajur*)
¼ cup deseeded tamarind (*imli*)
1 cup grated jaggery (*gur*)
1 tsp chilli powder
A pinch asafoetida (*hing*)
Salt to taste

1. Wash the dates and tamarind and place them in a saucepan.
2. Add the jaggery, chilli powder, asafoetida, salt and 4 cups of water and simmer for 20 to 25 minutes.
3. Cool and strain the mixture through a sieve.
4. Store refrigerated in an air-tight container and use as required.

Handy Tip: You can also purée the chutney in a food processor and then strain it through a sieve.

Garlic Chutney

A simple mixture of chilli and garlic that can be stored for upto five days in the refrigerator.

Preparation Time: 10 minutes.
Cooking Time: Nil.
Makes 1 cup.

½ cup garlic cloves, peeled
6 tbsp chilli powder
1 tsp lemon juice
Salt to taste

1. Combine all the ingredients and blend in a mixer to a coarse paste, using very little water.
2. Store refrigerated in an air-tight container and use as required.

Spicy Kachumber

A simple yet *chatpata kachumber* which goes well with any Indian delicacy and is made with common and readily-available salad ingredients.

Preparation Time: 10 minutes.
Cooking Time: Nil.
Serves 4.

1 cup sliced onions
1 cup thinly sliced cucumber
½ cup sliced tomatoes
½ tsp roasted cumin seeds (*jeera*) powder
¼ tsp chilli powder
Juice of ½ lemon
Salt to taste

Combine all the ingredients in a serving bowl and serve immediately.

Oriental
platter

Oriental starters are pick-up snacks that are incomplete without the famous Peanut Sauce and Sweet and Sour Dip. Like all starters, they fuel the gastronomic juices and make way for the main course! These pungent oriental starters are perfect for starting a meal on a winter's day, replete with spicy chit-chat with close friends!

The combination of starters included in this section includes *Baby Corn Fritters*, which are quite common yet extremely tasty and ever-welcome. Baby corn can be substituted with any other vegetable of your choice. *Sweet Corn Balls* are also extremely simple to make. The sweetness of the corn contrasts well with the spiciness of chilli powder. Peanut butter and lemon grass give a distinctly unique flavour to the *satay*. *Sesame Paneer* is a modification of sesame fingers -- a popular Chinese specialty. *Paneer* has been used instead of bread in this recipe.

Baby Corn Fritters

Sweet Corn Balls

Paneer, Mushroom and Capsicum Satay

Sesame Paneer

Peanut Sauce

Sweet and Sour Dip

Tomato Chilli Sauce

Kimchi

Baby Corn Fritters

Batter-fried baby corn strips served with Sweet and Sour Dip.
An all-time Chinese favourite!

Preparation Time: 10 minutes.
Cooking Time: 10 minutes.
Serves 4.

To be mixed into a thick batter

½ cup plain flour (*maida*)
1 tsp cornflour
½ cup buttermilk
1 tsp chilli powder
1 tsp garlic (*lehsun*) paste
A pinch soda bi-carb
Salt to taste

Other ingredients

1 cup baby corn, cut into halves vertically
1 tsp salt
Oil for deep-frying

1. Combine the baby corn and salt and mix well. Keep aside for 8 to 10 minutes. Drain out the excess water.
2. Heat the oil in a *kadhai* on a medium flame, dip the baby corn into the prepared batter and deep-fry till they are golden brown in colour from all sides.
3. Drain on absorbent paper and serve hot.

Sweet Corn Balls

This ever-popular Chinese starter is perked up by the use of authentic red curry paste.

Preparation Time: 10 minutes.
Cooking Time: 20 minutes.
Makes 10 balls.
Soaking Time: 10 minutes.

2 cups sweet corn kernels (*makai ke dane*)
2 tbsp red curry paste, recipe below
½ cup finely chopped spring onion greens
1 tbsp soya sauce
6 tbsp rice flour (*chawal ka atta)*
Salt to taste
Oil for deep-frying

To be ground to a smooth red curry paste

1 red chilli, soaked in warm water for 10 minutes and drained
1 cup chopped onions
1 tsp ginger-garlic (*adrak-lehsun*) paste
1 tsp chopped lemon grass (*hare chai ki patti*)
1 tsp chopped coriander (*dhania*)
¼ tsp coriander (*dhania*) powder
¼ tsp cumin seeds (*jeera*) powder
Salt to taste
A pinch of pepper powder

1. Blend the sweet corn in a mixer to a coarse paste.
2. Transfer it to a bowl, add the red curry paste, spring onion greens, soya sauce, sweet corn paste, rice flour and salt in a bowl and mix well.
3. Divide the mixture into 10 equal portions and shape each portion into a round ball..
4. Heat the oil in a *kadhai* on a medium flame, and deep-fry the balls till they are golden brown in colour from all sides. Drain on an absorbent paper and serve hot.

Paneer, Mushroom and Capsicum Satay

A vegetarian satay of *paneer*, mushrooms and capsicum marinated in yummy peanut sauce.

Preparation Time: 25 minutes.
Cooking Time: 15 minutes.
Makes 6 skewers.

For the peanut sauce

1 tsp oil
2 tbsp chopped onions
2 cloves garlic (*lehsun*)
2 tbsp peanut butter
1 tbsp brown sugar
½ cup coconut milk
1 stalk lemon grass (*hare chai ki patti*)
1 tsp chilli powder
½ tsp grated lemon rind
Salt to taste
1 tsp lemon juice

Other ingredients

2 cups *paneer* (cottage cheese), cut into 25 mm. (1") cubes
1 cup mixed capsicum (red, yellow and green), cut into 25 mm. (1") cubes
12 large mushrooms (*khumbh*)
1 cup onions, cut into 25 mm. (1") cubes
Oil for cooking

For the peanut sauce

1. Heat the oil in a pan, add the onions and garlic and sauté till the onions turn translucent.
2. Add all the remaining ingredients, except the lemon juice and simmer for 10 to 15 minutes.
3. Remove from the flame and discard the lemon grass.
4. Add the lemon juice and mix well. Keep aside to cool.

How to proceed

1. Combine ¾ of the peanut sauce with the *paneer*, capsicum, mushrooms and onions in a bowl and mix well. Keep aside to marinate for 20 minutes.
2. Thread the *paneer*, capsicum, mushrooms and onions on 6 wooden skewers.
3. Heat the oil on a non-stick *tava* (griddle) and cook the skeweres on all sides are golden brown.
   Serve hot.

Handy Tips

1. You can use any other vegetables of your choice.
2. You can also grill the satay on a barbecue grill.

Peanut Sauce

A sweet and spicy peanut dip flavoured with lemon grass and coconut. An indispensable accompaniment for Chinese starters.

Preparation Time: 15 minutes.
Cooking Time: 15 minutes.
Makes 1½ cups.

1 tsp oil
2 tbsp finely chopped onions
1 tsp chopped garlic (*lehsun*)
2 tbsp peanut butter
1 tbsp brown sugar
½ cup coconut milk
½ tsp lemon rind
1 stalk lemon grass (*hare chai ki patti*)
½ tsp deseeded and finely chopped whole dry Kashmiri red chillies
Salt to taste

1. Heat the oil in a pan, add the onions and garlic and sauté for 2 minutes.
2. Add all the remaining ingredients and ½ cup of water and simmer for 15 minutes.
3. Remove from the flame, cool and remove and discard the lemon grass before serving.

Handy Tip: If peanut butter is not available, you can use 2 tbsp of peanut powder mixed with 1 tbsp of oil.

Sweet and Sour Dip

Combine this sweet and tangy dip with any deep-fried Thai starter for a captivating combo!

Preparation Time: 10 minutes.
Cooking Time: 15 minutes.
Makes ½ cup.

¼ cup fresh tamarind pulp
½ cup jaggery, crumbled
½ tsp chilli powder
1 tsp honey
½ tsp salt

1. Combine the tamarind pulp, jaggery and chilli powder with 2 tbsp of water and simmer till the sauce reduces to half.
2. Cool and add the honey and salt and mix well.

Tomato-Chilli Sauce

Readymade tomato-chilli sauce is one of the best accompaniments to an Oriental platter. But if you want to try something very authentic, try the recipe of Khimchi page 49.

Khimchi

This crunchy sweet and spicy preparation is the first dish that arrives when you dine at a Chinese restaurant. Khimchi is a general term that refers to preserved vegetables (that are usually eaten in the winter when fresh vegetables are scarce). You can also use cucumber and carrot strips along with the cabbage. Just remember to adjust the other ingredients proportionately.

Preparation Time: 5 minutes.
Cooking Time: Nil.
Makes 1 cup.

1 cup cabbage, cut into 25 mm. (1") cubes
1 tsp chilli powder
1 tbsp powdered sugar
1 tbsp white vinegar
1 tsp salt

1. Combine all the ingredients in a bowl and mix well.
2. Keep aside for at least an hour before serving.

Tips You can refrigerate this for a few days, stored in an air-tight container.

T*ikkis* are a great match for any party! While exotic *tikkis* are lovely to experiment with, there are times when you want to stick to the tested and avoid experiments for fear of 'flop shows' or to avert the risk of guests not liking new combinations.

Here is a platter of time-tested *tikkis* that will stand by you every single time!

Aloo Tikki, the ever-popular snack made of potatoes needs no introduction, nor does the famous *Hara Bhara Kebab* which entices with looks as much as with taste. *Papad Paneer Crispies* are succulent pieces of *paneer* coated *with* crispy *papads* that are deep-fried, a sure-shot hit with guests... never a failure. *Tilwale Aloo ka Tikka* are skinned baby potatoes with a tempering of sesame seeds. *Hare Chane ke Kebab* as the name says is *hare chane* combined with *paneer* and perked with basic India *masalas*.

All time favourites

Aloo Tikki

Papad Paneer Crispies

Hara Bhara Kebab

Hare Chane ke Kebab

Tilwale Aloo ka Tikka

Tandoori Roti

Garlic Tomato Chutney

Coriander Garlic Chutney

Aloo Tikki

The all time favourite *Aloo Tikki* is a hit with kids and grownups alike!

Preparation Time: 5 minutes.
Cooking Time: 10 minutes.
Makes 8 tikkis.

1 cup boiled, peeled and mashed potatoes
½ cup boiled and mashed green peas
1 tbsp chopped coriander (*dhania*)
½ tsp chilli powder
1 tsp *chaat masala*
1 tsp lemon juice
Salt to taste
Oil for cooking

1. Combine all the ingredients in a bowl and mix well.
2. Divide the mixture into 8 equal portions and shape each portion into a round, flat *tikki*.
3. Heat a non-stick pan on a medium flame and cook each *tikki*, using a little oil, till both sides are golden brown in colour.
4. Drain on an absorbent paper and serve hot.

Papad Paneer Crispies

An unusual preparation of *paneer* that has been rolled in crushed raw *papad* before frying.

Preparation Time: 5 minutes.
Cooking Time: 7 minutes.
Makes 16 crispies.

16 *paneer* (cottage cheese) cubes [25 mm. (1")]
2 tbsp red garlic *chutney*
2 raw *papads*
¼ cup plain flour (*maida*)
Salt to taste
Oil for deep-frying

1. Slice the *paneer* cubes into 2 halves.
2. Apply a little garlic chutney on ½ of the *paneer* cubes. Sandwich with the remaining *paneer* cubes. Keep aside.
3. Grind the *papads* in a blender to a coarse powder. Keep aside.
4. Combine the flour with salt and ¼ cup of water to make a thin batter.
5. Coat the sandwiched *paneer* cubes with the flour batter and then roll them in powdered *papad*.
6. Heat the oil in a *kadhai* on a medium flame and deep-fry a few *paneer* pieces at a time, till they are golden brown in colour from all sides. Drain on absorbent paper and serve hot.

Hara Bhara Kebab

A tried and tested recipe for one of the most popular vegetarian *kebabs* in the world!

Preparation Time: 10 minutes.
Cooking Time: 20 minutes.
Makes 8 kebabs.
Soaking Time: 1 hour.

¼ cup *chana dal* (split Bengal gram)
25 mm. (1") piece ginger (*adrak*)
2 tsp grated garlic (*lehsun*)
2 tsp finely chopped green chillies
1 cup blanched, drained and roughly chopped spinach (*palak*)
½ cup boiled green peas
½ cup grated *paneer* (cottage cheese)
1 tsp *chaat masala*
¼ tsp *garam masala*
Salt to taste
Bread crumbs for rolling
Oil for deep-frying

1. Clean, wash and soak the *chana dal* for 1 hour.
2. Drain, add the ginger, garlic, green chillies and ¾ cup of water and pressure cook for 2 to 3 whistles or until the *dal* is cooked.
3. Allow the steam to escape before opening the lid. Drain out and discard any excess water.
4. Add the spinach, green peas and cooked *dal* mixture and blend in a mixer to a coarse paste without using any water.
5. Add the *paneer*, *chaat masala*, *garam masala* and salt and mix well.
6. Divide the mixture into 8 equal portions and shape each portion into a flat, tear drop shaped *kebab*.
7. Roll the *kebabs* in the bread crumbs so that they are evenly coated on both sides.
8. Heat the oil in a *kadhai* on a medium flame and deep-fry the *kebabs*, till they are golden brown in colour from both sides. Drain on absorbent paper and serve hot.

Hare Chane ke Kebab

Hara chana when combined with *paneer* and flavoured with *garam masala* makes a delicious *kebab* that everyone is sure to love!

Preparation Time: 15 minutes.
Cooking Time: 10 minutes.
Makes 12 kebabs.
Soaking Time: Overnight.

1 cup *hara chana* (whole green gram)
¼ tsp soda-bi-carb
1 cup grated *paneer* (cottage cheese)
½ cup finely chopped onions
1 tsp finely chopped ginger (*adrak*)
2 tsp finely chopped green chillies
3 tbsp chopped coriander (*dhania*)
1 tsp *garam masala*
1 tsp coriander (*dhania*) powder
1 tsp lemon juice
Salt to taste
Melted butter for cooking

1. Clean wash and soak the *hara chana* overnight.
2. Drain, add the soda-bi-carb and 2 cups of water and pressure cook for 3 to 4 whistles or until the *hara chana* is cooked.
3. Allow the steam to escape before opening the lid. Drain and discard any excess water.
4. Combine the *hara chana* with all the remaining ingredients in a bowl and mix well.
5. Divide the mixture into 12 equal portions and shape each portion into a flat, oval *kebab*.
6. Cook the *kebabs* on a *tava* (griddle), using a little butter till both sides are golden brown in colour. Serve hot.

Tilwale Aloo ka Tikka

Here's a smashing combination of baby potatoes and sesame seeds that is jazzed up with a combination of Indian spices.

Preparation Time: 10 minutes.
Cooking Time: 15 minutes.
Serves 4.

2 tbsp oil
¼ tsp cumin seeds (*jeera*)
½ tsp mustard seeds (*rai / sarson*)
4 to 6 curry leaves (*kadi patta*)
2 tsp ginger-green chilli paste
16 parboiled baby potatoes, peeled
¼ tsp turmeric powder (*haldi*)
Salt to taste
2 tbsp roasted sesame seeds (*til*)
1 tsp lemon juice

For the garnish
1 tbsp chopped coriander (*dhania*)
1 tsp finely chopped green chillies

1. Heat the oil in a non-stick pan and add the cumin seeds, mustard seeds and curry leaves.
2. When the seeds crackle, add the ginger-green chilli paste and stir for some time.
3. Add the potatoes, turmeric powder and salt and sauté for 4 to 5 minutes.
4. Add ½ cup of water and cook on a slow flame till all the moisture has evaporated and the potatoes are cooked.
5. Remove from the flame, add the sesame seeds and lemon juice and mix well.

Serve hot garnished with coriander and green chillies.

Tandoori Rotis

Hmmm, the flavour imparted by the traditional clay *tandoor* is unbeatable, but you can make do with an inverted pressure pan and a gas stove instead!

Preparation Time: 20 minutes.
Cooking Time: 15 minutes.
Makes 8 rotis.

1 cup whole wheat flour (*gehun ka atta*) or plain flour (*maida*)
1 tsp crumbled fresh yeast
1 tsp sugar
1 tsp finely chopped garlic (*lehsun*)
½ tsp salt
1 tsp oil
Whole wheat flour (*gehun ka atta*) for rolling
1 tsp oil for greasing

1. Combine all the ingredients, except the oil, in a bowl and knead into soft dough, using enough water until it is smooth and elastic.
2. Add the oil and knead again.
3. Cover the dough with a wet muslin cloth and allow it prove till it doubles in volume (approx. 15 to 20 minutes).
4. Press the dough lightly to remove the air.
5. Divide the dough into 8 equal portions.
6. Roll out each portion into a 125 mm. (5") diameter circle using little flour.
7. Remove the lid of the pressure cooker and lightly grease the insides of the bottom with oil.
8. Heat upside down over an open flame.
9. Apply a little water on one side of each *tandoori roti* and stick the wet side on the inside of the heated bottom of the pressure cooker.
10. Again turn the bottom of the pressure cooker upside down and cook till brown spots appear on the surface of the *tandoori roti* and it peels away easily.
11. You can stick 3 to 4 *tandoori rotis* on the inside of the pressure cooker at a time.
    Serve hot.

Garlic Tomato Chutney

Two common ingredients, brought together with other complementary ingredients, create magic in this recipe!

Preparation Time: 10 minutes.
Cooking Time: 15 minutes.
Makes ¾ cup (approx. 11 tbsp).

2 whole dry Kashmiri red chilies, soaked
1 tsp olive oil or oil
¼ cup chopped spring onion whites
6 to 8 large cloves garlic (*lehsun*), finely chopped
Salt to taste
1 cup finely chopped tomatoes
1 tbsp finely chopped coriander (*dhania*)
1 tbsp finely chopped spring onion greens

1. Drain the soaked chillies and chop them finely.
2. Heat the oil in a deep pan, add the spring onion whites and garlic and sauté over a slow flame for 4 to 5 minutes till they are lightly brown.
3. Add the chillies and salt and for 30 second sauté again.
4. Add the tomatoes and cook for 10 to 12 minutes over a slow flame till the tomatoes are soft and can be mashed lightly.
5. Cool completely, add the coriander and spring onion greens and mix well.
   Serve chilled or at room temperature.

Coriander Garlic Chutney

A simple but luscious *chutney* that will leave you wishing for more!

Preparation Time: 5 minutes.
Cooking Time: Nil.
Makes ½ cup (approx. 7 tbsp).

½ cup chopped fresh green garlic (*hara lehsun*), including the greens
1 cup finely chopped coriander (*dhania*)
1 tsp lemon juice
1 tbsp *daria* (roasted Bengal gram)
½ cup water
Salt to taste

Combine all the ingredients and blend in a mixer till smooth.
Serve immediately.

Continental *platter*

***K**ebabs* seem so indigenous that it is tough to think of *kebabs* that aren't *desi*! Sounds cheesy? That is what it is! Here is a platter of cheese-laden continental *kebab* recipes.

Broccoli and cheese balls are a great duo for making *tikkis*. There is a piece of cheese in each *tikki* which melts when deep fried, ultimately melting in your mouth. Remember to use only mozzarella cheese as it imparts a good texture.

Brinjal Fritters are made of grated mozzarella sandwiched between two slices of brinjal, dipped in a batter and deep-fried. Well, they tasted nice but looked bad! So, I have placed them on a wooden satay sticks interspersed with carrot slices and topped with olives.

Potato Epice is a kind of *tikki* that gains an exotic flavour from the herbs. Aloo cheese is of course a universal favourite. Serve with a Fruit and Vegetables, Salad, Barbeque Sauce and Bread Rolls to complete the continental experience.

Broccoli and Cheese Balls

Brinjal Fritters

Potato Epice

Aloo Cheese Croquettes

Whole Wheat Brown Bread Rolls

Fruit and Vegetable Salad

Barbeque Sauce

Broccoli and Cheese Balls

delicacy that is sure to steal the hearts of young and old alike hopefully, there shouldn't be a war between the camps for more!

Preparation Time: 10 minutes.
Cooking Time: 15 minutes.
Makes 15 balls.

1 tbsp oil
½ cup finely chopped onions
1 tsp finely chopped garlic (*lehsun*)
2 tsp finely chopped green chillies
1 cup finely chopped broccoli
2 tbsp cornflour
¾ cup boiled, peeled and mashed potatoes
Salt to taste
15 cubes of mozzarella cheese [cut into 25 mm (1") cube]
Bread crumbs for rolling
Oil for deep-frying

1. Heat the oil in a pan, add the onions, garlic and green chillies and sauté for 2 minutes.
2. Add the broccoli and sauté for another 4 to 5 minutes till the broccoli is almost cooked.
3. Remove from the flame, add the cornflour, potatoes and salt and mix well.
4. Divide the mixture into 15 equal portions and shape each portion into a flat round.
5. Press a little in the centre of each round to make a depression. Place a mozzarella cheese cube in the centre of each round and roll again to form a ball.
6. Roll each ball in bread crumbs in such a way that the balls are evenly coated from all sides.
7. Heat the oil in a *kadhai* on a medium flame and deep-fry the balls, till they are golden brown in colour from all sides. Drain on absorbent paper and serve hot.

Brinjal Fritters

A unique preparation of chewy cheese sandwiched between brinjal slices. While serving, string the fritters and carrot slices on a satay stick, or top with an olive.

Preparation Time: 5 minutes.
Cooking Time: 10 minutes.
Serves 4.

To be mixed together into a thick batter

5 tbsp plain flour (*maida*)
5 tbsp cornflour
Salt to taste
1 tsp chilli powder
Water as required

Other ingredients

3 tbsp grated mozzarella cheese
3 tbsp grated processed cheese
2 tsp finely chopped green chillies
2 cups thinly sliced long brinjals (*baingan / eggplant*)
2 tsp dry mango powder (*amchur*), salt and
1 tsp chilli powder for sprinkling
Oil for frying

1. Combine the mozzarella cheese, processed cheese and green chillies in a bowl and mix well. Keep aside.
2. Place a little of this cheese mixture on one slice of brinjal. Place another brinjal slice over it so that the mixture is sandwiched between the two slices.
3. Repeat with the remaining ingredients to make more fritters.
4. Heat the oil in a *kadhai* on a medium flame, dip a few fritters at a time in the batter and deep-fry till they are golden brown in colour from all sides.
5. Drain on an absorbent paper, sprinkle dry mango powder, salt and chilli powder on them and serve hot.

Potato Epice

This ready-in-a-jiffy preparation of buttery potatoes tossed with mixed herbs, paprika and assorted bell peppers is one of my favourites!

Preparation Time: 10 minutes.
Cooking Time: 5 to 7 minutes.
Serves 4.

2 tbsp butter
½ cup assorted capsicum (red, yellow and green), cut into 50 mm. (2") strips
1 cup boiled and potatoes, cut into 25 mm. (1") x 50 mm. (2") strips (batons)
½ cup boiled peeled sweet potatoes, cut into 25 mm. (1") x 50 mm. (2") strips (batons)
1 tbsp dried mixed herbs
2 tsp dry red chilli flakes (*paprika*)
Salt to taste

For the garnish
1 tsp butter

1. Heat the butter in a pan, add the capsicum and sauté for 2 to 3 minutes.
2. Add the potatoes, sweet potatoes, mixed herbs, red chilli flakes and salt and sauté for 3 to 4 minutes or till the potatoes and sweet potatoes turn golden brown.
   Serve hot topped with butter.

Handy tip: Dried mixed herbs are readily available at most leading provision stores.

Aloo Cheese Croquettes

Potato rolls stuffed with chilli-garlic sauce are great as a snack for your kids and as a scrumptious starter while entertaining.

Preparation Time: 10 minutes.
Cooking Time: 10 minutes.
Makes 6 croquettes.

To be mixed into a cheesy stuffing

2 tbsp grated mozzarella cheese
2 tbsp grated cheese
3 tbsp chilli-garlic sauce

Other ingredients

4 cups boiled, peeled and mashed potatoes
Salt to taste
½ tsp freshly ground pepper
Oil for deep-frying

1. Combine the potatoes, salt and pepper in a bowl and mix well.
2. Divide this mixture into 6 equal portions and shape each portion into a small round.
3. Press a little in the centre of each round to make a depression. Place 1 tsp of the cheesy filling in the depression and again shape them into cylindrical croquettes.
4. Heat the oil in a *kadhai* on a medium flame, and deep-fry the croquettes till they are golden brown in colour from all sides. Drain on an absorbent paper and serve hot.

Whole Wheat Brown Bread Rolls

It would be wise to serve bread rolls with a platter of continental *kebabs* to make it a holistic experience!

Preparation Time: 2 minutes.
Cooking Time: Nil.
Makes 20 rolls.
Baking Temperature and Time :
200°C (400°F) for 5 minutes.
150°C (300°F) for 10 minutes.

125 gm whole wheat flour (*gehun ka atta*)
125 gm plain flour (*maida*)
2 tsp (10 gm) fresh yeast
¾ tsp sugar
1 tsp butter
¾ tsp salt

1. Combine the wheat flour and plain flour in a bowl and make a well in the centre.
2. Add the yeast, sugar and a little warm water.
3. Wait for at least 4 to 5 minutes or until bubbles come on top.
4. Add the butter and salt, mix well and make a soft dough by adding some more warm water.
5. Knead the dough for 2 minutes.
6. Keep under a wet cloth for 20 minutes. Knead again for 1 minute.
7. Shape into small loaves and put on a well-greased baking tray
8. Keep the tray in a closed cupboard for 25 minutes or until double in size.
9. Bake in a hot oven at 200°C (400°F) for 5 minutes. Then reduce the temperature to 150°C (300°F) and bake a further 10 minutes.
10. Remove from the tin and brush on top with butter and serve hot.

Fruit and Vegetable Salad

A light tropical salad with a delicious dressing, this is a great starter for summer as well as winter evenings!

Preparation Time: 20 minutes.
Cooking Time: Nil.
Serves 4.

1 cup orange segments
1 cup apple slices
½ cup banana slices
½ cup pineapple cubes
½ cup sweet lime segments
2 beetroots, chopped or sliced
½ cup lettuce, torn into pieces
2 tbsp pomegranate (*anar*)
2 tbsp roasted and crushed peanuts

To be mixed into a dressing (in a bottle)
2 tbsp salad oil
1 tbsp white vinegar
2 tsp orange squash
Salt and freshly ground pepper to taste

Combine all the ingredients in a bowl, add the dressing and toss well.
Serve immediately

Barbeque Sauce

A spicy and yummy treat!

Preparation Time: 20 minutes.
Cooking Time: 20 minutes.
Makes ¾ cup.

2 tsp vinegar
1 tsp lemon juice
½ cup water
½ cup finely chopped onions
2 tbsp sugar
¼ cup butter
½ tsp freshly ground pepper
½ cup tomato ketchup
1 tsp salt
2 tbsp Worcestershire sauce (readily available in the market)
¼ tsp dry red chilli flakes (*paprika*)
1 piece charcoal and 1 tsp butter for smoking

1. Combine all the ingredients in a pan and bring to boil. Allow it to simmer for about 10 to 12 minutes. Keep aside.
2. Heat the charcoal over a gas till it is red hot and place it in a small bowl.
3. Place this bowl in the saucepan that contains the sauce, pour the butter over the coal and cover it immediately. Leave aside for 5 to 10 minutes.
4. Remove the bowl containing the coal and discard.

Serve warm.

The Mughal era reminds one of all things grand and royal. Normally, Mughlai *kebabs* are predominantly meat-based but we have modified the traditional *kebabs* and made them vegetarian for you. On seeing the menu, you will be surprised by the use of ingredients like *rajma*, lotus stem etc. This is indeed a special platter fit for the finest dining, and the choice of exotic ingredients contributes to the perfection. A bowl of dry fruits could also be added to this as an accompaniment. *Khamiri roti*, a sweetish saffron topped delight is surely a highlight of this platter.

Farmaishi Suran

Aloo Tuk

Vegetable Shikampuri Kebab

Rajma Galouti Kebab

Nadier Palak Tikki

Khamiri Roti

Radish Chutney

Nawabi *platter*

Farmaishi Suran

Yam manifests as a scrumptious and tangy *kebab* that competes healthily with the other interesting *kebabs* on this extremely interesting platter!

Preparation Time: 10 minutes.
Cooking Time: 10 minutes.
Makes 8 kebabs.

1 tbsp coriander (*dhania*) seeds
2 whole dry Kashmiri red chillies, broken into pieces
½ cup grated yam (*suran*)
¼ cup grated *paneer* (cottage cheese)
½ tsp dry mango powder (*amchur*)
Salt to taste
Cornflour for rolling
Oil for deep-frying

1. Combine the coriander seeds and Kashmiri red chillies in a pan and dry roast them for 1 minute.
2. Remove from the flame and grind to a coarse powder using a mortar-pestle (*khalbhatta*). Keep aside.
3. Combine all the remaining ingredients in a bowl, add the ground spice and mix well.
4. Divide the mixture into 8 equal portions and shape each portion each portion into a round ball.
5. Roll each *kebab* in cornflour in such a way that the *kebabs* are evenly coated from all sides.
6. Heat the oil in a *kadhai* on a medium flame, and deep-fry the balls till they are golden brown in colour from all sides. Drain on an absorbent paper and serve hot.

Aloo Tuk

A Sindhi specialty that has gained popularity in households all over the world!

Preparation Time: 10 minutes.
Cooking Time: 20 minutes.
Serves 4.

To be mixed together for the *masala* powder

1 tsp dry mango powder (*amchur*)
½ tsp chilli powder
¼ tsp black pepper powder
Salt to taste

Other ingredients

2½ cups baby potatoes (unpeeled)
Salt to taste
Oil for deep-frying

1. Wash the baby potatoes very well and parboil them in salted water. Drain and keep aside.
2. Heat the oil in a *kadhai* on a medium flame and deep-fry the potatoes till they are cooked. Drain on absorbent paper and allow them to cool for a while.
3. Press each potato between the palms of your hands to flatten them and deep-fry again in the same hot oil till they are golden brown in colour from both sides.
4. Drain on absorbent paper and then place them on a serving plate.
5. Sprinkle the *masala* powder on top and toss well.

   Serve immediately.

Vegetable Shikampuri Kebab

A combination of finely ground vegetables, *paneer* and khoya, this is a truly royal experience!

Preparation Time: 15 minutes.
Cooking Time: 15 minutes.
Makes 20 kebabs.

1 cup roughly chopped and parboiled mixed vegetables (carrots, cauliflower, French beans etc.)
¾ cup boiled, peeled and mashed potatoes
1 tbsp ghee
1 tsp caraway seeds (*shahjeera*)
½ tsp finely chopped ginger (*adrak*)
1 tsp finely chopped green chillies
¼ tsp turmeric powder (*haldi*)
1 tsp chilli powder
Salt to taste
2 tbsp chopped mint leaves (*phudina*)
2 tbsp finely chopped coriander (*dhania*)
¼ cup bread crumbs
½ tsp cardamom (*elaichi*) powder
¼ cup grated *paneer* (cottage cheese)
¼ cup khoya (*mava*)
½ cup chopped and browned onions
A pinch freshly ground pepper
Oil for cooking

1. Combine the mixed vegetables and the potatoes in a mixer and grind till coarse. Keep aside.
2. Heat the ghee in a pan and add the caraway seeds.
3. When the seeds crackle, add the ginger, green chillies, the ground mixture, turmeric powder, chilli powder and salt and sauté for 2 to 3 minutes.
4. Add the mint leaves and coriander and sauté for another minute.
5. Remove from the flame and allow the mixture to cool.
6. Add the *paneer*, khoya and browned onions and bread crumbs and mix well.
7. Divide the mixture into 20 equal portions and shape each portion into a flat, oval *kebab*.
8. Heat a non-stick pan and cook each *kebab*, using a little oil, till both sides are golden brown in colour or cook on a barbeque till done.
9. Drain on an absorbent paper and serve hot.

Rajma Galouti Kebab

A delectable vegetarian version of the traditional galouti *kebab*, where meat has been replaced with *rajma*.

Preparation Time: 10 minutes.
Cooking Time: 30 minutes.
Makes 5 kebabs.

Oil for deep-frying
¾ cup sliced onions
2 tbsp ghee
2 tbsp finely chopped ginger (*adrak*)
1½ tsp finely chopped green chillies
¼ tsp turmeric powder (*haldi*)
½ cup *paneer* (cottage cheese)
¾ cup soaked, boiled and lightly mashed *rajma* (kidney beans)
½ cup boiled, peeled and mashed potatoes
1 tbsp chopped coriander (*dhania*)
Salt to taste
½ tsp *garam masala*
1 tbsp oil

1. Heat the oil in a *kadhai* on a medium flame and deep-fry the onions till they are golden brown. Drain on absorbent paper and keep aside.
2. Heat the ghee in a pan, add the ginger and green chillies and sauté for 30 seconds.
3. Add all the remaining ingredients except the oil and cook for 3-4 minutes.
4. Divide the mixture into 5 equal portions and shape each portion into flat, round *kebabs*.
5. Heat the oil in a *kadhai* on a medium flame and deep-fry the *kebabs* till golden brown in colour from both sides. Drain on absorbent paper and serve hot.

Nadier Palak Tikki

A traditional tikki made with lotus roots, potatoes and spinach, combined with a tangy green paste and delicately flavoured with fennel powder.

Preparation Time: 5 minutes.
Cooking Time: 5 minutes.
Makes 30 tikkis.

3 lotus stems, cleaned and grated
1 cup boiled, peeled and mashed potatoes
½ cup finally chopped spinach (*palak*)
¼ cup chopped coriander (*dhania*)
½ cup finely chopped onions
1 tsp fennel seeds (*saunf*) powder
½ tsp *garam masala*
2 tsp finely chopped green chillies
2 tbsp cornflour
Salt to taste
Mustard oil (*rai ka tel*) for deep-frying

1. Combine all the ingredients in a bowl and mix well.
2. Divide the mixture into 30 equal portions and shape each portion into a small oval *tikki.*
3. Heat the mustard oil in a *kadhai* on a medium flame and deep-fry the *tikkis* till they are golden brown in colour from both sides.
4. Drain on an absorbent paper and serve hot.

Khamiri Roti

Khamiri roti is the Mughals' closest answer to leavened bread. Khamir, which means yeast, is used to prepare this *roti*, thus making it thick and spongy. *Khamiri roti* tastes great with nearly any *subzi* and can even be eaten with just a bit of butter. Paired with Dal Makhni and Nawabi Paneer or the choicest of *kebabs*, it makes a dining experience you would be ready to give your right arm for!

Preparation Time: minutes.
Cooking Time: 5 minutes.
Makes 10 rotis.
Baking Temperature: 200°C (400°F).
Baking Time : 10 to 12 minutes.

1 tsp (5 gms) fresh yeast, crumbled
2 cups whole wheat flour (*gehun ka atta*)
½ tsp sugar
½ tsp carom seeds (*ajwain*)
½ tsp salt
Whole wheat flour (*gehun ka atta*) for rolling
Oil for greasing
A few strands of saffron (*kesar*) soaked in
¼ cup of milk for brushing

1. Dissolve the yeast and sugar in 2 tbsp of lukewarm water and leave aside for 10 minutes or until the yeast begins to ferment.
2. Combine all the ingredients and knead into a hard dough using enough warm water (approx. ½ cup). Knead well (approx. 4 to 5 minutes). Keep the dough aside for 2 to 3 hours covered with a damp muslin cloth.
3. Divide the dough into 10 equal portions and roll out each portion into a circle of 100 mm. (4") diameter with the help of a little flour.
4. Place the *rotis* on a greased baking tray and bake in a pre-heated oven at 200°C (400°F) for 5 to 6 minutes.
5. Brush each roti with saffron mixture and serve hot.

Radish Chutney

If tomatoes and coriander seem common place, treat your guests to this tangy radish chutney.

Preparation Time: 8 to 10 minutes.
Cooking Time: Nil.
Makes 1½ cups.

1 cup grated white radish (*mooli*)
¼ cup chopped mint leaves (*phudina*)
¼ cup chopped coriander (*dhania*)
3 green chillies
½ cup fresh curds (*dahi*)
Salt to taste

For the garnish
2 tbsp grated white radish (*mooli*)

Combine all the ingredients and blend in a mixer to a smooth paste.
Keep refrigerated till use. Serve chilled garnished with white radish.

Low Cal Kebab *platter*

*K*ebabs and low cal? The terms don't seem to go together, but I am not joking! You can now enjoy a low cal *kebab* platter if you have the time to slow-cook them. All you need to take care of is to avoid the use of high calorie ingredients like khoya, cheese etc. and substitute these with a variety of veggies, low cal milk products like curds and *paneer*, and cook the *kebabs* using very minimal oil. Also note that since these are made using less oil, you should serve them immediately lest they turn soggy and unappetising!

Mint and Masoor Tikki, as the name suggests is a mint flavoured tikki mixed with *masoor* and *paneer* to add a dose of calcium to your diet. *Seven Grain Tikki* is another healthy option that provides a protein boost. If you don't have a particular grain, just skip it, without any worries!

Suhana Hara Kebab is a unique combination of paneer, sweet corn and green peas coated with healthy corn flakes instead of bread crumbs or semolina. *Mexican Kebab* comprises veggies on a satay stick spiked with a sweet-spicy marinade.

The accompaniments have also been carefully formulated to avoid excess calories. The *Carrot Garlic Chutney* and *Chunky Vegetable Dip* also devoid of high cal ingredients like coconut and groundnut. *Brown bread* is also made with whole wheat and not maida, thus ensuring that you feel satiated for several hours, avoiding binge-eating!

Mint and Masoor Tikki
Seven Grain Tikki
Mexican Kebab
Suhana Hara Kebab
Carrot Garlic Chutney
Chunky Vegetable Dip
Whole Wheat Pav

Mint and Masoor Tikki

Whole masoor has been combined with bread crumbs and paneer and flavoured with loads of mint. A minty fresh delight!

Preparation Time: 10 minutes.
Cooking Time: 25 minutes.
Makes 8 tikkis.
Soaking Time: Overnight.

NUTRUTIVE VALUES PER TIKKI
52 CALORIES 0.7 GM FAT

¾ cup whole *masoor* (whole red lentils)
¾ cup finely chopped mint leaves (p*hudina*)
2 tsp ginger-green chilli paste
2 tbsp brown bread crumbs
½ cup grated low fat *paneer*
(cottage cheese), page 96
Salt to taste
2 tsp oil for cooking

1. Clean, wash and soak the *masoor* overnight.
2. Drain, add 2 cups of water and pressure cook for 2 to 3 whistles till the *masoor* is soft and slightly overcooked, but not mashed.
3. Allow the steam to escape before opening the lid.
4. Drain the *masoor* and discard any excess water. Coarsely mash the *masoor* with a potato masher.
5. Add all the remaining ingredients and mix well.
6. Divide the mixture into 8 equal portions and shape each portion into a small long, flat *tikki.*
7. Pierce a wooden satay stick through each *tikki* and cook each *tikki* on a hot non-stick *tava* (griddle) on a medium flame, using 1/8 tsp of oil, till both sides are golden brown in colour from both sides. Drain on an absorbent paper and serve hot.

Seven Grain Tikki

A delicious and healthy treat made from seven different grains, and of course, the goodness of all of these!

Preparation Time: 15 minutes.
Cooking Time: 10 minutes.
Makes 12 tikkis.
Soaking Time: 3 hours.

NUTRUTIVE VALUES PER TIKKI
77 CALORIES 1.1 GM FAT

2 tbsp *masoor dal* (split red lentils)
½ cup *chana dal* (split Bengal gram)
1 cup mixed sprouts (*moong, matki, chana* etc.)
3 to 4 green chillies
12 mm. (½") piece ginger (*adrak*)
1 tbsp fennel seeds (*saunf*)
2 cloves garlic (*lehsun*)
Salt to taste
1 cup boiled, peeled and mashed potatoes
½ cup mashed low fat *paneer*
(cottage cheese), page 96
½ cup chopped coriander (*dhania*)
1 cup finely chopped spring onions (with leaves)
2 tsp toasted sesame seeds (*til*)
and 2 tbsp wheat germ for rolling
1½ tsp oil for cooking

1. Clean, wash and soak the *chana dal* and *masoor dal* in water for 3 hours.
2. Drain and combine both the *dals* along with mixed the sprouts, green chillies, ginger, fennel seeds, garlic and salt and blend in a mixer to a coarse paste.
3. Add the mashed potatoes, mashed *paneer*, coriander and spring onions and mix well.
4. Divide the mixture into 12 equal portions and shape each portion into a square, flat *tikki*.
5. Roll the *tikkis* in the sesame seeds and wheat germ till they are evenly coated on both sides.
6. Pierce a wooden satay stick through each *tikki* and cook each *tikki* on a hot non-stick *tava* (griddle) on a medium flame, using 1/8 tsp of oil, till both sides are golden brown in colour from both sides. Drain on an absorbent paper and serve hot.

Mexican Kebab

Here is a combination of capsicum, babycorn, *paneer* and mushrooms marinated in a unique mixture of cocoa powder, curds, oregano and garlic. Go ahead and indulge in the exotic taste!

Preparation Time: 15 minutes.
Cooking Time: 10 minutes.
Serves 4.

NUTRUTIVE VALUES PER KEBAB
38 CALORIES 1.5 GM FAT

To be mixed into a marinade

2 tsp cocoa powder
2 tsp chilli powder
1 tbsp curds (*dahi*)
2 tsp crushed garlic (*lehsun*)
½ tsp oregano
1 tsp oil
Salt and pepper to taste

Other ingredients

¼ cup capsicum (red, green and yellow), cut into 25mm. (1") cubes
½ cup blanched baby corn, cut into vertical halves
1 cup low fat *paneer* (cottage cheese), page 96, cut into 25mm. (1") pieces
½ cup blanched mushrooms (*khumbh*)
½ cup onions, cut into 25 mm. (1") pieces

1. Combine the capsicum, baby corn, *paneer*, mushrooms and onions with the marinade and keep aside for 4 to 5 hours.
2. Thread them on individual wooden satay sticks and cook the *kebabs* over the grill or over a charcoal barbeque till they are evenly browned on all sides (approx. 3 to 4 minutes).
   Serve hot.

Suhana Hara Kebab

A simple *kebab* of *paneer* and green peas that can be eaten at any time of the day.

Preparation Time: 10 minutes.
Cooking Time: 10 minutes.
Makes 20 kebabs.

NUTRUTIVE VALUES PER KEBAB
57 CALORIES 0.7 GM FAT

1 cup grated low fat *paneer* (cottage cheese), page 96
1 cup boiled green peas
1 cup boiled and crushed sweet corn (*makai ke dane*)
½ cup boiled, peeled and mashed potatoes
½ tsp cardamom (*elaichi*) powder
Salt to taste
1 tbsp cornflour mixed in ½ cup of water
¼ cup crushed cornflakes for coating
2½ tsp oil for cooking

1. Combine the *paneer,* green peas, corn, potatoes, cardamom powder and salt in a bowl and mix well.
2. Divide the mixture into 20 equal portions and shape each portion into a round, flat *kebab*. Keep aside.
3. Dip the *kebabs* in the cornflour mixture and roll them in cornflakes and cook each *kebab* on a hot non-stick *tava* (griddle) on a medium flame, using 1/8 tsp of oil, till both sides are golden brown in colour from both sides. Drain on an absorbent paper and serve hot.

Carrot Garlic Chutney

This *chutney* is a great way of including fibre-rich carrots and cholesterol-lowering garlic to your meals.

Preparation Time: 30 minutes.
Cooking Time: Nil.
Makes ½ cup (approx. 7 tbsp).

NUTRUTIVE VALUES PER TBSP
13 CALORIES 0.7 GM FAT

1 cup thickly grated carrots
2 tbsp chopped garlic (*lehsun*)
2 tsp chilli powder
¼ tsp lemon juice
1 tsp oil
Salt to taste

1. Combine all the ingredients and blend in a mixer to a fine paste.
2. Store refrigerated in an air-tight container and use as required.

Chunky Vegetable Dip

This protein rich dip is low in fat yet filled with a wealth of nutrients and a medley of enticing flavours.

Preparation Time: 15 minutes.
Cooking Time: Nil.
Makes 1½ cups.

NUTRUTIVE VALUES PER TBSP
13 CALORIES 0 GM FAT

2 tbsp low fat milk
¾ cup grated low fat *paneer* (cottage cheese), page 96
2 tbsp chopped celery
¼ cup chopped carrots
¼ cup chopped capsicum
2 tbsp chopped spring onion greens
2 tbsp chopped tomatoes
¼ cup chopped cucumber
1 tbsp chopped parsley
Salt to taste

1. Combine all ingredients in a bowl and mix well.
2. Keep refrigerated for 2 hours.
   Serve chilled.

▪ Whole Wheat Pav ▪

For a satiating meal, serve this platter with whole wheat pavs available in the bakery.

BASIC RECIPE

Low Fat Paneer

Low fat *paneer* that is made from low fat milk and low fat curds contains more protein and calcium than full fat *paneer*.

Preparation Time: 10 minutes.
Cooking Time: 10 minutes.
Makes 100 grams (approx. ¾ cup).

2 cups low fat milk

1 cup beaten low fat curds (*dahi*)

1. Put the milk to boil in a saucepan. When it starts boiling, add the low fat curds and mix well.
2. Remove from the heat and stir gently until the milk curdles.
3. Strain the curdled milk through muslin cloth, bring the edges of the cloth together, tie and hang for about ½ hour to allow the whey to drain out. Use as required.

Handy tips:

1. If the milk has not curdled completely in step 2, heat the mixture for a little more time.
2. Whey is very nutritious so try using it innovatively instead of discarding it.
3. It can be used instead of water for kneading dough or can be added to juices and buttermilk.